D1809219

greek

greek

RECIPES FROM THE HEART OF THE MEDITERRANEAN

introduction by
jim antoniou

LORENZ BOOKS

This edition published by Lorenz Books
an imprint of Anness Publishing Limited
Hermes House, 88–89 Blackfriars Road, London SE1 8HA

© Anness Publishing Limited 1998, 1999

This edition distributed in Canada by Raincoast Books
8680 Cambie Street, Vancouver, British Columbia V6P 6M9

All rights reserved. No part of this publication may be reproduced, stored in a retrieval system, or transmitted in any way or by any means, electronic, mechanical, photocopying, recording or otherwise, without the prior written permission of the copyright holder.

ISBN 0-7548-0253-1

Publisher Joanna Lorenz
Senior Cookery Editor Linda Fraser
Project Editor Zoe Antoniou
Designer Ian Sandom
Illustrations Madeleine David
Photographers William Adams-Lingwood, Karl Adamson, Edward Allwright, James Duncan, Michelle Garrett, Amanda Heywood, Tim Hill, Don Last, Patrick McLeavey and Michael Michaels
Stylists Frances Cleary, Nicola Fowler, Michelle Garrett, Teresa Goldfinch, Carole Handslip, Cara Hobday, Clare Louise Hunt, Maria Kelly, Sarah Maxwell, Kirsty Rawlings and Fiona Tillett
Recipes Carla Capalbo, Jacqueline Clark, Frances Cleary, Roz Denny, Matthew Drennan, Joanna Farrow, Christine France, Silvana Franco, Carole Handslip, Judy Jackson, Soheila Kimberley, Patricia Lousada, Sarah Maxwell, Janice Murfitt, Angela Nilsen, Jenny Stacey and Liz Trigg
Home Economists Lucy McKelvie, Jane Stevenson and Elizabeth Wolf-Cohen

Cover:
Photographer Nicki Dowey; *Home Economist* Emma Patmore;
Design Wilson Harvey Marketing and Design

Printed and bound in Singapore
1 3 5 7 9 10 8 6 4 2

For all recipes, quantities are given in both metric and imperial measures, and, where appropriate, measures are also given in standard cups and spoons. Follow one set, but not a mixture, because they are not interchangeable.

Olive grove on frontispiece and boats on page 7 courtesy of Michelle Garrett.
Scenic photographs on pages 6 and 9 courtesy of Jim Antoniou.

CONTENTS

INTRODUCTION

The Greeks enjoy the simple things in life: sun, sea and fresh air. They also like to eat well, and after centuries of experimenting, they have developed an exquisite flavour to their food that is recognized and enjoyed throughout the world. The country's geographic setting is such that its cuisine has benefitted from the Orient as well as from Europe, and this has created an array of delicious tastes that are unique. The main ingredients used in Greek cooking are olive oil, fresh tomatoes and lemons.

Food and drink are at the centre of the social life of the Greeks. They are known to relax and amuse themselves for hours around the table, where eating and drinking provide the inspiration for many a philosophical discussion about life, politics or even football.

While sitting and talking in the Mediterranean sunshine, the Greeks are often seen sipping coffee, or a drink, usually with *meze*, which is perhaps the most famous feature of their cuisine. A *meze* is a small portion of something delicious – it can be anything from a creamy dip to a plate of elaborately stuffed vegetables, or perhaps even just a few fresh olives. This may also be accompanied by the rhythmic sound of the *bazouki*, the Greek equivalent to the guitar, which can often be heard late into the night.

A *meze* often also proves to be a convenient way to serve unexpected guests at the table. Greek hospitality towards strangers is an age old tradition that dates back to Homeric times. Odysseus, while travelling light and incognito from island to island, was often treated with many generous offerings of culinary hospitality. *Philoxenia*, literally "a love of strangers", remains a national virtue in Greece and an accepted way of life in the country areas. In villages, a place is always found for a stranger at the table. During such a meal, a guest is likely to be offered a choice of meat or a particular fruit from the host's own plate – such a gesture should not be refused.

Churches (left) can be seen in every village in Greece. Another common sight is a fishing boat (right) in the early hours.

Fresh vegetables and fruit are important ingredients in Greek cooking.

One essential feature of Greek cuisine is the use of fresh ingredients. Meat and fish are often simply grilled, and served with fresh herbs and lemon juice, accompanied by a refreshing Greek salad. Such cooking methods have evolved around the abundance of fish, available from the coastlines around mainland Greece and the islands.

Chicken and lamb are the most commonly eaten meats, due to the rather rugged terrain which is unsuited to raising cattle, especially during the long hot summertime. But even so, these more common meats were traditionally seen as a rare luxury, particularly in ancient times, which may explain their emphasis in Homer's epics. Odysseus was rarely offered fish, in spite of its obvious abundance. Meat is often cooked in a similar way to fish, on a barbecue or spit. A family's roasting lamb sends out an inviting spicy aroma from one garden to the next.

In contrast to these simple recipes, there are also many national dishes that can take days to make. A lengthy preparation process is an important part of the appreciation of food, and it plays a prominent role in various festivities. In the spring, the Greek Orthodox Easter is dominated by *magiritsa*, a soup to break the fast after the midnight mass, and traditional *tsoureki*, a bread with a red dyed egg in the centre, symbolizing the blood of Christ. Dyed eggs of various colours are used at this time to decorate the table. They are also used to play fun and competitive egg-cracking games.

A door to a local shop, painted in the bright sea-blue colour that Greece is famous for.

Fresh herbs are plentiful in Greece.

In rural areas, where many families rely upon the cultivation of land, people tend to eat what is in season. In winter, Avgolemono Soup (made with egg and lemon) is tangy and refreshingly light. In the autumn, black-eye beans served with greens is a popular dish, or chicken with *pilafi* (rice cooked in the juice of the meat). *Horta* is extremely popular, a wild green not unlike spinach in taste and equally strong in iron content. Okra is also a favourite vegetable. Parts of Greece are also renowned for particular products, such as olives from Kalamata, honeydew melons from Argos and grapes from Crete.

A common addition to the Greek table is an alcoholic drink, which is an important part of the enjoyment of food. Indeed, Greeks regard all people who drink without eating as not quite civilized. Perhaps the most famous drink is ouzo, an aniseed tasting spirit that turns cloudy when water is added. Greece is also responsible for retsina, a resinated wine with an unusual, strong taste.

Breakfast is simply coffee, similar to Turkish coffee, and perhaps a slice of bread or a few biscuits. Lunch starts about two in the afternoon and lasts for an hour or so. The evening meal is taken at around ten o'clock and can last well into the night. Fruit is plentiful according to the season, with an abundance of melons, apricots and peaches and a choice of over three hundred grape varieties. There are also many sweet pastries to choose from, although these are more often seen as a speciality rather than a common dessert.

Above all, the secret of enjoying a Greek meal is not to rush it, but rather to sit long over each course. When the mood takes you, stand up and dance the *syrtaki*, taking in the exciting music, the beautiful scenery and the company of friends, which all add to the unforgettable experience of eating Greek food.

AVGOLEMONO SOUP

This soup is made with egg, lemon and chicken stock. It is simple to make and has few ingredients, but is full of flavour.

INGREDIENTS

50g/2oz/1 cup thread egg noodles
1 litre/1¾ pints/4 cups hot chicken stock
60ml/4 tbsp chopped fresh parsley
30ml/2 tbsp lemon juice
1 egg
1 lemon, for slicing
salt and freshly ground black pepper

SERVES 4

COOK'S TIP

After adding the lemon juice and egg mixture, do not allow the soup to boil, or the eggs will curdle. The soup should thicken until it is a rich and creamy texture.

---

1 Place the noodles and stock in a saucepan. Bring to the boil. Simmer for 5 minutes, or until the noodles are tender. Remove from the heat, add the parsley and stir to mix.

2 Beat the lemon juice and egg together in a mixing bowl and add 30ml/2 tbsp of the hot soup. Pour the mixture back into the saucepan and stir until just thickened.

3 Cut the lemon into slices, cutting each one in half. Season the soup, then add the lemon slices and serve immediately.

LENTIL SOUP

The beautifully rich colour of this soup, known as *faki*, comes from the red wine, tomatoes and brown lentils. It tastes just as good as it looks.

INGREDIENTS

225g/8oz/1 cup brown lentils
1 litre/1¾ pints/4 cups chicken stock
50ml/2 fl oz/¼ cup dry red wine
675g/1½lb ripe tomatoes, peeled, seeded
and chopped, or 400g/14oz can
chopped tomatoes
1 carrot, sliced
1 onion, chopped
1 celery stick, sliced
1 garlic clove, crushed
1.5ml/¼ tsp ground coriander
10ml/2 tsp chopped fresh basil, or
2.5ml/½ tsp dried basil
1 bay leaf
75g/3oz/6 tbsp freshly grated
Parmesan cheese (optional)

SERVES 6

VARIATION

For a more substantial soup, add about 175g/6oz/1 cup finely chopped cooked ham for the last 10 minutes of cooking.

1 Rinse the lentils and discard any discoloured ones and any stones.

2 Combine the lentils, chicken stock, wine, tomatoes, carrot, onion, celery, garlic and 250ml/8fl oz/1 cup water in a large saucepan. Add the ground coriander, fresh or dried basil and bay leaf.

3 Bring to the boil and reduce the heat to low. Cover the pan and simmer for about 20–25 minutes, or until the lentils are just tender, stirring occasionally.

4 Discard the bay leaf. Ladle the soup into six soup bowls and sprinkle each one with the grated cheese, if you like.

DOLMADES

The exact ingredients of this traditional Greek dish vary from region to region. Vine leaves and cooked rice are essential, however.

INGREDIENTS
250g/9oz fresh vine leaves
30ml/2 tbsp olive oil
1 large onion, finely chopped
250g/9oz minced lamb
75g/3oz/½ cup cooked rice
30ml/2 tbsp chopped fresh parsley
30ml/2 tbsp chopped fresh mint
30ml/2 tbsp snipped fresh chives
3–4 spring onions, finely chopped
juice of 2 lemons
30ml/2 tbsp tomato purée (optional)
30ml/2 tbsp sugar
salt and freshly ground black pepper
yogurt and pitta bread, to serve (optional)

SERVES 4–6

1 Blanch the vine leaves in boiling water for 1–2 minutes to soften them.

2 Heat the olive oil in a large frying pan and fry the onion for a few minutes until slightly softened. Add the lamb and fry over a moderate heat until well browned, stirring frequently. Season with salt and pepper.

3 Stir the cooked rice, chopped herbs, spring onions and the juice of one of the lemons into the lamb. Add the tomato purée, if using, and then knead the mixture with your hands until thoroughly blended.

4 Place a vine leaf on a chopping board with the vein side up. Place 15ml/1 tbsp of the lamb mixture on the vine leaf and fold the stem end over the meat. Fold the sides in towards the centre and then fold over to make a neat parcel. Continue until all the filling has been used up.

5 Line the base of a large saucepan with several unstuffed leaves and arrange the rolled leaves in tight layers on top. Stir the remaining lemon juice and the sugar into about 150ml/¼ pint/⅔ cup water and pour over the leaves. Place a heat resistant plate over the Dolmades to keep them in shape. Cover the pan tightly and cook over a very low heat for 2 hours, checking occasionally and adding a little extra water should the pan begin to boil dry. Serve warm or cold with yogurt and warm pitta bread, if liked.

COOK'S TIP
If using preserved vine leaves, soak them overnight in cold water and then rinse several times before use.

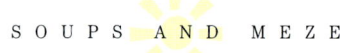

HUMMUS

This chick-pea and sesame seed dip is good with crackers, warm pitta bread or raw vegetables. The tahini – sesame seed paste – is available from delicatessens and health food stores. Try to make twice the quantity if you can, as Hummus freezes well.

INGREDIENTS
225g/8oz/1¼ cups chick-peas,
soaked overnight
115g/4oz/½ cup tahini paste
2 garlic cloves, crushed
juice of 1–2 lemons
60ml/4 tbsp olive oil
salt
cayenne pepper and flat leaf parsley,
to garnish
pitta bread, to serve

SERVES 4

COOK'S TIP
You can use a can (400g/14oz) of chick-peas in this recipe as the final result will be just as good. Simply omit the soaking and boiling and just drain, reserving the liquid for use later. Season carefully if extra salt has been added to the can.

1 Drain the chick-peas and cook them in fresh boiling water for 10 minutes. Reduce the heat and simmer for about 1 hour or until soft. Drain the chick-peas, reserving the cooking liquid.

2 Put the chick-peas into a food processor or blender and add the tahini paste, garlic and a little lemon juice. Process until smooth. Season and add enough cooking liquid to process until creamy. Add more lemon juice or liquid as the Hummus stiffens after resting.

3 Spoon the Hummus on to plates, swirl it with a knife and drizzle with olive oil. Sprinkle with cayenne pepper, garnish with parsley and serve with pitta bread.

TARAMASALATA

This delicious speciality makes an excellent starter to any meal. It is perhaps one of the most famous Greek dips.

INGREDIENTS

115g/4oz smoked mullet roe
2 garlic cloves, crushed
30ml/2 tbsp grated onion
60ml/4 tbsp olive oil
4 slices white bread, crusts removed
juice of 2 lemons
30ml/2 tbsp milk or water
freshly ground black pepper
warm pitta bread, to serve

SERVES 4

1 Place the smoked roe, garlic, onion, oil, bread and lemon juice in a blender or food processor and process until smooth.

2 Add the milk or water and process again for a few seconds. (This will give the Taramasalata a creamier texture.)

3 Pour the Taramasalata into a serving bowl, cover with clear film and chill for 1–2 hours before serving. Sprinkle the dip with freshly ground black pepper and serve with warm pitta bread.

COOK'S TIP
Since the roe of grey mullet is expensive, smoked cod's roe is often used instead for this dish. It is paler than the burnt-orange colour of mullet roe but is still very good.

AUBERGINE DIP

This is a delicious velvet-textured dip that can be simply spread on slices of bread, or eaten as an accompaniment to more strongly flavoured dishes. It is called *melitzanasalata*.

INGREDIENTS

1 large aubergine
1 small onion
2 garlic cloves
30ml/2 tbsp olive oil
45ml/3 tbsp chopped fresh parsley
75ml/5 tbsp crème fraîche
red Tabasco sauce, to taste
juice of 1 lemon, to taste
salt and freshly ground black pepper
crusty white bread or toast, to serve

SERVES 4

COOK'S TIP
The aubergine can be roasted in the oven at 200°C/400°F/Gas 6 for about 20 minutes, if preferred.

1 Preheat the grill. Place the whole aubergine on a baking sheet and grill it for 20–30 minutes, turning occasionally, until the skin is blackened and wrinkled, and the aubergine feels soft when squeezed.

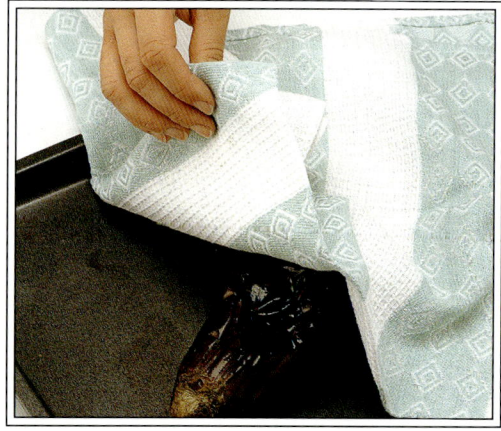

2 Cover the aubergine with a clean dish towel and leave to cool for 5 minutes.

3 Finely chop the onion and garlic. Heat the oil in a frying pan and cook the onion and garlic for 5 minutes until softened but not browned.

4 Peel the skin from the aubergine. Mash the flesh into a pulpy purée.

5 Stir in the onion mixture, parsley and crème fraîche. Add Tabasco, lemon juice and seasoning. Serve on toast or crusty white bread with a garnish of your choice.

VEGETABLE FRITTERS WITH TZATZIKI

Spicy deep fried aubergine and courgette slices served with a creamy yogurt and dill dip make a good, simple party starter or an excellent side dish.

INGREDIENTS
1 large aubergine, thickly sliced
2 courgettes, thickly sliced
1 egg white
40g/1½oz/4 tbsp plain flour
10ml/2 tsp ground coriander
10ml/2 tsp ground cumin
olive or vegetable oil, for frying
salt and freshly ground black pepper
paprika and a fresh dill sprig, to garnish

FOR THE DIP
½ cucumber, roughly grated
225g/8oz/1 cup Greek-style yogurt
15ml/1 tbsp olive oil
10ml/2 tsp fresh lemon juice
30ml/2 tbsp chopped fresh dill
15ml/1 tbsp chopped fresh mint
1 garlic clove, crushed

SERVES 4–6

1 Layer the aubergine and courgettes in a colander and sprinkle with salt. Leave for 30 minutes, rinse and pat dry.

2 Mix the dip ingredients together. Season, spoon into a bowl and set aside.

3 Beat the egg white in a bowl. In a separate bowl, mix the flour, coriander and cumin with seasoning.

4 Dip the vegetables first into the egg white then into the seasoned flour and set aside.

5 Heat about 2.5cm/1in of oil in a deep frying pan until quite hot, then fry the vegetables, a few at a time, until they are golden and crisp.

6 Drain and keep warm while you fry the remaining pieces. Serve them warm on a platter with some of the Tzatziki dip lightly sprinkled with paprika, and garnish with a dill sprig.

KEFTEDES

These spiced lamb kebabs are delicious. The cool mint dressing complements them well.

INGREDIENTS
675g/1½ lb lamb
1 onion, quartered
3–4 fresh parsley sprigs
2–3 fresh coriander sprigs
1–2 fresh mint sprigs
2.5ml/½ tsp ground cumin
2.5ml/½ tsp mixed spice
5ml/1 tsp paprika
salt and freshly ground black pepper
fresh mint, to garnish
pitta bread, to serve (optional)

FOR THE MINT DRESSING
30ml/2 tbsp finely chopped fresh mint
90ml/6 tbsp natural yogurt

MAKES 12–14

1 Roughly chop the lamb, place in a food processor or blender and process until smooth. Transfer to a plate.

2 Add the onion, parsley, coriander and mint to the processor or blender and process until finely chopped. Add the lamb together with the spices and seasoning and process again until very smooth. Transfer to a bowl and chill for about 1 hour.

3 To make the dressing, blend the chopped fresh mint with the yogurt and chill until required.

4 Mould the meat mixture into small sausage shapes and skewer them with wooden or metal kebab sticks. Preheat a grill or barbecue.

5 Cook the Keftedes for 5–6 minutes, turning once. Place on a dish and serve immediately with the mint dressing, garnished with mint, and accompanied by warm pitta bread, if liked.

SPANAKOPITES

hese spinach and feta cheese triangles are delicious and much simpler to make than they look.

INGREDIENTS
30ml/2 tbsp olive oil
2 shallots, finely chopped
450g/1lb frozen spinach, thawed
115g/4oz/½ cup feta cheese, crumbled
40g/1½oz/⅓ cup walnut pieces, chopped
1.5ml/¼ tsp grated nutmeg
4 large or 8 small sheets filo pastry
115g/4oz/½ cup butter or
margarine, melted
salt and freshly ground black pepper

MAKES 20

VARIATION
For an alternative filling, you can omit the spinach and shallots. Use 375g/12oz crumbled goat's cheese instead of the feta cheese, and 50g/2oz/½ cup toasted pine nuts instead of the walnuts. Mix the goat's cheese with the olive oil and 15ml/1 tbsp chopped fresh basil. Assemble as above.

---

1 Preheat the oven to 200°C/400°F/Gas 6. Heat the olive oil in a heavy-based frying pan. Add the shallots and cook for about 5 minutes, until softened.

2 Squeeze all the liquid out of the spinach and add to the shallots. Cook over a high heat, stirring, for 5 minutes or until all excess moisture has evaporated.

3 Transfer the spinach mixture to a bowl and allow to cool. Stir in the feta and nuts. Season with nutmeg, salt and pepper.

4 Lay a filo sheet on a flat surface. (Keep the remaining filo covered with a damp dish towel to prevent it drying out.) Brush with some of the butter or margarine. Lay a second filo sheet on top of the first. With scissors, cut the layered filo pastry lengthwise into strips 8cm/3in wide.

5 Place a spoonful of the spinach mixture at the end of the strip of filo pastry. Fold a bottom corner of the pastry over the filling to form a triangle, then continue folding over the pastry strip to the other end. Fill and shape the triangles until all of the ingredients are used.

6 Set the triangles on baking sheets and brush with melted butter. Bake the filo triangles in the preheated oven for about 10 minutes, or until they become crispy and golden brown. Serve hot as a starter, snack or light lunch.

DEEP FRIED WHITEBAIT

A spicy coating on these fish gives this favourite dish, *marides*, a crunchy bite. It can also be served as a starter.

INGREDIENTS
115g/4oz/1 cup plain flour
2.5ml/¹/₂ tsp paprika
2.5ml/¹/₂ tsp ground cayenne pepper
pinch of salt
1.1kg/2¹/₂lb whitebait, thawed if frozen
vegetable oil, for deep frying
lemon wedges, to serve

SERVES 6

1 Mix together all the dry ingredients in a large mixing bowl.

2 Place the whitebait in the bowl with the spicy flour mixture and coat thoroughly.

3 Heat the oil in a large, heavy-based saucepan until it reaches a temperature of 190ºC/375ºF. Fry the whitebait in batches for 2 minutes, or until the fish is golden and crispy.

4 Drain well on absorbent kitchen paper and serve hot with lemon wedges.

DEEP FRIED PRAWNS AND SQUID

Prawns (*garides*) and squid (*calamari*) are a favourite Greek combination, but any mixture of seafood can be used in this dish.

INGREDIENTS
vegetable oil, for deep frying
600g/1lb 5oz cooked prawns, shelled and deveined
600g/1lb 5oz squid (about 12) cleaned and cut into bite-size pieces
115g/4oz/1 cup flour
lemon wedges, to serve

FOR THE BATTER
2 egg whites
30ml/2 tbsp olive oil
15ml/1 tbsp white wine vinegar
90g/3¹/₂oz/scant 1 cup flour
10ml/2 tsp baking soda
75g/3oz/¹/₃ cup cornflour
salt and freshly ground black pepper

SERVES 6

1 Make the batter in a large mixing bowl by beating the egg whites, olive oil and vinegar together lightly with a wire whisk. Beat in the dry ingredients and whisk until well blended. Beat in 250ml/8fl oz/1 cup water, a little at a time. Cover the bowl, and allow to stand for 15 minutes.

2 Heat the oil for deep frying in a heavy-based saucepan to about 185°C/360°F, or until a small piece of bread sizzles as soon as it is dropped in.

3 Coat the prawns and squid pieces in the flour, shaking off any excess. Dip them quickly into the batter. Fry in small batches for about 1 minute, stirring with a slotted spoon to keep the pieces from sticking to each other.

4 Remove and drain on kitchen paper. Allow the oil to come back up to the correct temperature between batches. Sprinkle lightly with salt, and serve hot with lemon wedges.

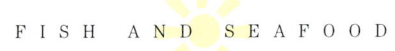
FISH PARCELS

Sea bass is good for this recipe, but you could also use small whole trout or white fish fillet such as cod or haddock.

INGREDIENTS

4 pieces sea bass fillet or 4 whole small
sea bass, about 450g/1lb each
oil, for brushing
2 shallots, thinly sliced
1 garlic clove, chopped
15ml/1 tbsp capers
6 sun-dried tomatoes, finely chopped
4 black olives, stoned and thinly sliced
grated rind and juice of 1 lemon
5ml/1 tsp paprika
salt and freshly ground black pepper
fresh parsley, to garnish
crusty bread, to serve

SERVES 4

1 Preheat the oven to 200°C/400°F/Gas 6. Clean the fish, if whole. Cut four large squares of double-thickness foil, large enough to enclose the fish. Brush each square with a little oil.

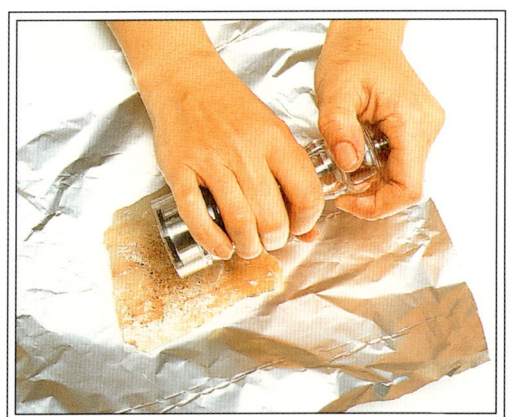

2 Place a piece of fish in the centre of each piece of foil and season well with salt and pepper.

3 Scatter over the shallots, garlic, capers, tomatoes, olives and grated lemon rind. Sprinkle with the lemon juice and paprika.

4 Fold the foil over to enclose the fish loosely, sealing the edges. Bake in the preheated oven for 15–20 minutes. Place the contents of the parcels on serving plates with crusty bread, and garnish with parsley.

STUFFED CALAMARI

alamari, or baby squid, are quick to cook, but do turn and baste them often and don't overcook them.

INGREDIENTS
500g/1¼ lb baby squid, cleaned
1 garlic clove, crushed
3 plum tomatoes, skinned and chopped
8 sun-dried tomatoes in oil, drained and chopped
60ml/4 tbsp chopped fresh basil, plus extra to garnish
60ml/4 tbsp fresh white breadcrumbs
45ml/3 tbsp olive oil
15ml/1 tbsp red wine vinegar
salt and freshly ground black pepper
lemon juice and wedges, to serve

SERVES 4

1 Remove the tentacles from the squid and roughly chop them. Leave the main part of the squid whole.

2 Mix together the tentacles, garlic, plum tomatoes, sun-dried tomatoes, fresh basil, and breadcrumbs. Stir in 15ml/1 tbsp of the olive oil and all of the red wine vinegar. Season well with salt and pepper. Meanwhile, soak some wooden cocktail sticks in water for about 10 minutes before use to prevent them from burning.

3 With a teaspoon, fill the squid with the stuffing mixture. Secure the open ends with the cocktail sticks.

4 Brush with the remaining oil. Cook under a medium-hot grill for 4–5 minutes, turning often. Sprinkle with lemon juice and basil. Serve with lemon wedges.

COD PLAKI

G enerally in Greece, fish is treated very simply but this recipe is a little more involved, flavouring the fish with onions, herbs and tomatoes.

INGREDIENTS

300ml/¹/₂ pint/1¹/₄ cups olive oil
2 onions, thinly sliced
3 large well-flavoured tomatoes,
roughly chopped
3 garlic cloves, thinly sliced
5ml/1 tsp sugar
5ml/1 tsp chopped fresh dill
5ml/1 tsp chopped fresh mint
5ml/1 tsp chopped fresh celery leaves
15ml/1 tbsp chopped fresh parsley
6 cod steaks
juice of 1 lemon
salt and freshly ground black pepper
fresh dill, mint or parsley, to garnish

SERVES 6

1 Heat the oil in a large frying pan or flameproof dish. Add the onions and cook until pale golden. Add the tomatoes, garlic, sugar, dill, mint, celery leaves and parsley with 300ml/½ pint/1¼ cups water. Season with salt and pepper, then simmer, uncovered, for 25 minutes or until the liquid has reduced by a third.

2 Add the fish steaks and cook gently for 10–12 minutes or until the fish is just cooked. Remove from the heat and add the lemon juice. Cover and leave to stand for about 20 minutes before serving. Arrange the cod in a serving dish and spoon the sauce over. Garnish with herbs and serve either warm or cold.

OCTOPUS AND RED WINE STEW

 ctopus and red wine blend beautifully to create this unusual and tasty Greek meal.

INGREDIENTS
900g/2lb prepared octopus
450g/1lb onions, sliced
2 bay leaves
450g/1lb ripe tomatoes
60ml/4 tbsp olive oil
4 garlic cloves, crushed
5ml/1 tsp caster sugar
15ml/1 tbsp chopped fresh oregano
or rosemary
30ml/2 tbsp chopped fresh parsley
150ml/¼ pint/⅔ cup red wine
30ml/2 tbsp red wine vinegar
chopped fresh herbs, to garnish
warm bread, to serve

SERVES 4

1 Put the octopus in a saucepan of gently simmering water with a quarter of the onions and both bay leaves. Cook for 1 hour.

2 While the octopus is cooking, plunge the tomatoes into boiling water for about 30 seconds, then refresh in cold water. Peel away the skins and chop roughly.

3 Drain the octopus. Using a sharp knife, cut it into bite-size pieces and discard the head.

4 Heat the oil in a saucepan and fry the octopus, the remaining onions and the garlic for 3 minutes. Add the tomatoes, sugar, oregano or rosemary, parsley, wine and vinegar and cook, stirring, for 5 minutes until pulpy.

5 Cover the saucepan and cook over the lowest possible heat for about 1½ hours until the sauce is thickened and the octopus is tender. Transfer to a serving dish, garnish with fresh herbs and serve with warm bread.

> COOK'S TIP
> Unless you're happy to clean and prepare an octopus for this dish, buy one that's ready for cooking. Most big supermarkets and fishmongers should be able to supply them.

RED MULLET WITH TOMATOES

For flavour and ease of preparation, this dish simply cannot be beaten. It is cooked using just one pan.

INGREDIENTS
4 red mullet, about 175–200g/6–7oz each
450g/1lb tomatoes, peeled, or
400g/14oz can plum tomatoes
60ml/4 tbsp olive oil
60ml/4 tbsp finely chopped fresh parsley
2 garlic cloves, finely chopped
120ml/4fl oz/¹/₂ cup white wine
4 thin lemon slices, cut in half
salt and freshly ground black pepper

SERVES 4

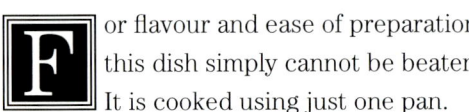

1 Scale and clean the fish without removing the liver. Wash and pat dry with kitchen paper.

2 Chop the tomatoes into small pieces. Heat the oil in a saucepan or flameproof casserole large enough to hold the fish in one layer. Add the parsley and garlic and sauté for 1 minute. Stir in the tomatoes and cook for 15–20 minutes over a moderate heat. Season with salt and pepper.

3 Add the fish to the tomato sauce and cook over a moderate to high heat for 5 minutes. Add the wine and the lemon slices. Bring the sauce back to the boil and cook for about 5 minutes more. Turn the fish over and cook for 4–5 minutes more. Remove the fish to a warmed serving platter and keep warm until needed.

VARIATION
Small sea bass may be substituted.

4 Boil the sauce for 3–4 minutes to reduce it slightly. Spoon it over the fish. Serve, decorated with the cooked lemon slices.

GRILLED SEA BASS WITH FENNEL

resh sea bass is a popular fish in Greece. The herbs and lemon juice create a delicious flavour here.

INGREDIENTS

1 sea bass, about 1.75kg/4–4¹/₂lb, gutted and cleaned
60–90ml/4–6 tbsp olive oil
10–15ml/2–3 tsp fennel seeds
2 large fennel bulbs, trimmed and thinly sliced (reserve any fronds)
olive oil, for brushing
salt and freshly ground black pepper
juice of ¹/₂ lemon, to serve

SERVES 6

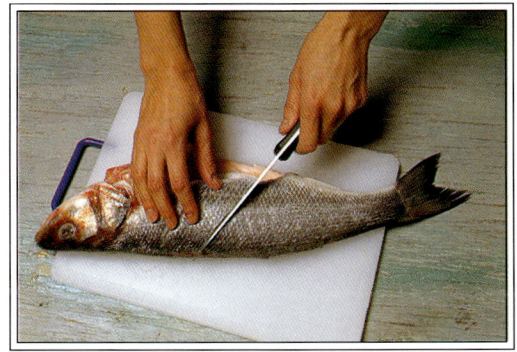

1 With a sharp knife, make three or four deep cuts in both sides of the fish. Brush the fish with olive oil and season with salt and pepper.

2 Sprinkle the fennel seeds evenly in the stomach cavity and in the cuts. Set the fish aside in a cool place while you prepare and cook the fennel.

3 Preheat the grill to a medium heat. Put the slices of fennel in a flameproof dish or on the grill rack and brush with oil. Grill for about 4 minutes on each side until tender. Transfer the slices to a large platter.

4 Place the fish on the oiled grill rack and position about 10–13cm/4–5in away from the heat. Grill for 10–12 minutes on each side, brushing with oil occasionally.

5 Transfer the fish to the platter on top of the fennel. Garnish with fennel fronds. Sprinkle with lemon juice and serve at once.

CHICKEN KEBABS

hicken kebabs are a great favourite all over Greece. They are ideal for summer barbecues.

INGREDIENTS
1 large onion, grated
2 garlic cloves, crushed
120ml/4fl oz/½ cup olive oil
juice of 1 lemon
5ml/1 tsp paprika
2–3 saffron strands, soaked in
15ml/1 tbsp boiling water
2 young chickens
salt and freshly ground black pepper
pitta bread, to serve

SERVES 6–8

1 Mix the onion, garlic, olive oil, lemon juice, paprika and saffron, and season with salt and pepper.

2 Cut the chicken into small pieces, removing the bone if preferred, and place in a shallow bowl. Pour the marinade over the chicken, turning the chicken so that all the pieces are covered evenly. Cover the bowl loosely with clear film and leave in a cool place to marinate for at least 2 hours.

VARIATION
You could remove the boneless chicken from the metal skewers and serve it in pitta bread as a sandwich accompanied by a garlicky yogurt sauce.

3 Thread the chicken on to long kebab sticks. The kebabs can be barbecued or cooked under a moderately hot grill for 10–15 minutes, or until the juices run clear when the meat is pierced. Turn them every now and then. Serve with warm pitta bread.

CHICKEN AND OLIVES

 beautiful combination of summer flavours makes this a perfect recipe for informal entertaining.

INGREDIENTS
30ml/2 tbsp olive oil
1 chicken, about 1.5kg/3–3½lb
1 large onion, sliced
15ml/1 tbsp grated fresh root ginger
3 garlic cloves, crushed
5ml/1 tsp paprika
250ml/8fl oz/1 cup chicken stock
2–3 saffron strands, soaked in
15ml/1 tbsp boiling water
4–5 spring onions, chopped
15–20 black and green olives, stoned
juice of ½ lemon
salt and freshly ground black pepper
rice and mixed salad, to serve (optional)

SERVES 4

1 Heat the oil in a large saucepan or flameproof casserole and sauté the chicken on all sides until golden.

2 Add the onion, fresh ginger, garlic, paprika and seasoning, and continue frying over a moderate heat, coating the chicken with the mixture.

3 Add the chicken stock and saffron and bring to the boil. Cover and simmer gently for 45 minutes, or until the chicken is well done and the meat comes away from the bone easily.

4 Add the spring onions and cook for a further 15 minutes until the sauce is reduced to about 120ml/4fl oz/½ cup.

5 Add the black and green olives and the lemon juice to the saucepan, stir and continue to cook gently for approximately 5 minutes more.

6 Remove the chicken and place it on a large deep serving plate. Carefully pour over the sauce. Serve with rice and a mixed salad, if liked.

BARBECUED LAMB WITH POTATO SLICES

A traditional mixture of fresh herbs adds a summer flavour to this dish. It is designed for the barbecue, a common cooking method in Greece.

INGREDIENTS
1 leg of lamb, about 1.75kg/4–4½ lb
1 garlic clove, sliced
handful each of fresh flat leaf parsley, sage, rosemary and thyme sprigs
90ml/6 tbsp dry sherry
60ml/4 tbsp walnut oil
500g/1¼lb potatoes
salt and freshly ground black pepper

SERVES 4

1 Place the lamb on a board, smooth side downwards so that you can see where the bone lies. Using a sharp knife, make a long cut through the flesh down to the bone.

2 Scrape away the meat from the bone on both sides, until the bone is completely exposed. Remove the bone and cut away any sinews and excess fat.

3 Cut through the thickest part of the meat to enable it to open out as flat as possible. Make several cuts in the lamb with a sharp knife, and push slivers of garlic and some of the herb sprigs into them.

4 Place the meat in a bowl and pour over the sherry and oil. Chop about half the remaining herbs and scatter over the meat. Cover and leave to marinate in the fridge for at least 30 minutes.

5 Remove the lamb from the marinade and season. Place on a medium-hot barbecue and cook for 30–35 minutes, turning occasionally and basting with the reserved marinade. Alternatively, preheat the oven to 200°C/400°F/Gas 6, and place the lamb in an ovenproof dish in the oven. Cook in the same way.

6 Scrub the potatoes, then cut them into thick slices. Brush them with the marinade and place them around the lamb. Continue cooking for about 15–20 minutes, turning occasionally, until the meat and potatoes are golden brown. Serve at once.

COOK'S TIP
A leg of lamb is easier to cook if it is boned, or "butterflied", first.

PASTITSIO

This Greek version of a pasta bake makes an excellent main meal – it is both economical and filling.

INGREDIENTS

15ml/1 tbsp oil
450g/1lb/4 cups minced lamb
1 onion, chopped
2 garlic cloves, crushed
30ml/2 tbsp tomato purée
25g/1oz/¼ cup plain flour
300ml/½ pint/1¼ cups lamb stock
2 large tomatoes
115g/4oz/1 cup pasta shapes
450g/1lb/2 cups Greek-style yogurt
2 eggs
salt and freshly ground black pepper
crisp salad and crusty bread, to serve

SERVES 4

1 Heat the oil in a large saucepan and fry the lamb for 5 minutes. Add the onion and garlic and fry for a further 5 minutes.

2 Stir in the tomato purée and flour. Cook for 1 minute.

3 Stir in the lamb stock and season with salt and pepper to taste. Bring to the boil and cook gently for about 20 minutes.

4 Slice the tomatoes, place the meat mixture in an ovenproof dish and arrange the tomatoes on top. Preheat the oven to 190ºC/375ºF/Gas 5.

5 Cook the pasta shapes in boiling salted water for 8–10 minutes or until just tender. Drain well.

6 Mix together the pasta, yogurt and eggs. Spoon on top of the tomatoes and cook in the preheated oven for 1 hour. Serve with a crisp salad and crusty bread.

MOUSSAKA

ne of Greece's most famous dishes, this has now become a favourite all over the world.

INGREDIENTS
15ml/1 tbsp oil
225g/8oz/2 cups minced lamb
5ml/1 tsp ground cumin
1 red onion, chopped
25g/1oz/¼ cup plain flour
175ml/6fl oz/¾ cup lamb stock
30ml/2 tbsp tomato purée
15ml/1 tbsp chopped fresh oregano
1 aubergine, sliced
salt and freshly ground black pepper
Greek Salad, to serve

FOR THE SAUCE
25g/1oz/2 tbsp butter
25g/1oz/¼ cup plain flour
300ml/½ pint/1¼ cups milk
50g/2oz/½ cup freshly grated
Cheddar cheese
1 egg, beaten

SERVES 4

1 Heat the oil in a large saucepan and fry the lamb and cumin for 5 minutes.

2 Add the onion and fry for a further 5 minutes, stirring occasionally. Add the flour and cook for 1 minute. Stir in the stock, tomato purée and fresh oregano. Bring to the boil, then reduce the heat and cook for 30 minutes.

3 Cover a plate with kitchen paper. Lay the sliced aubergine on top and sprinkle with salt. Allow to stand for 10 minutes, then rinse thoroughly and pat dry. Preheat the oven to 180°C/350°F/Gas 4.

4 For the sauce, melt the butter in a saucepan, add the flour and cook for 1 minute. Gradually stir in the milk and add the grated cheese. Season well and bring to the boil, stirring continuously. Remove from the heat and stir in the egg.

5 Spoon the lamb mixture into a dish, lay the aubergine slices on top and spoon on the sauce. Cook in the preheated oven for about 45–60 minutes, until the top is golden. Serve with a fresh Greek Salad.

KLEFTIKO

For this recipe, marinated lamb steaks or chops are slow-cooked to develop an unbeatable, meltingly tender flavour. The dish is sealed, like a pie, with a flour dough lid to trap succulence and flavour, although a tight-fitting foil cover, if less attractive, will serve equally well.

INGREDIENTS
juice of 1 lemon
15ml/1 tbsp chopped fresh oregano
4 lamb leg steaks or chump chops
with bones
30ml/2 tbsp olive oil
2 large onions, thinly sliced
2 bay leaves
150ml/¼ pint/⅔ cup dry white wine
225g/8oz/2 cups plain flour
salt and freshly ground black pepper
boiled potatoes, to serve (optional)

SERVES 4

COOK'S TIP
They are not absolutely essential for this dish, but lamb steaks or chops with bones will provide lots of additional flavour.

1 Mix together the lemon juice, oregano and salt and pepper, and brush over both sides of the lamb steaks or chops. Leave to marinate for at least 4 hours or overnight.

2 Preheat the oven to 160°C/325°F/Gas 3. Drain the lamb, reserving the marinade, and pat dry with kitchen paper. Heat the oil in a frying pan and fry the lamb over a high heat until browned on both sides.

3 Transfer the lamb to a shallow pie dish. Scatter the sliced onions and bay leaves around the lamb, then pour over the white wine and the reserved marinade.

4 Mix the flour with sufficient water to make a firm dough. Moisten the rim of the pie dish. Roll out the dough on a floured surface and use to cover the dish so that it is tightly sealed.

5 Bake for 2 hours, then break away the dough crust and serve the lamb hot, with boiled potatoes, if liked.

LAMB SAUSAGES WITH TOMATO SAUCE

The Greek name for these delicious sausages is *soudzoukakia*. They make a rich and tasty dish.

INGREDIENTS
50g/2oz/1 cup fresh breadcrumbs
150ml/¼ pint/⅔ cup milk
675g/1½lb/6 cups minced lamb
30ml/2 tbsp grated onion
3 garlic cloves, crushed
10ml/2 tsp ground cumin
30ml/2 tbsp chopped fresh parsley
flour, for dusting
60ml/4 tbsp olive oil
salt and freshly ground black pepper
flat leaf parsley, to garnish

FOR THE SAUCE
600ml/1 pint/2½ cups passata
5ml/1 tsp sugar
2 bay leaves
1 small onion, peeled

SERVES 4

1 In a mixing bowl, combine the fresh breadcrumbs and the milk. Then add the minced lamb, onion, garlic, ground cumin and parsley and season with salt and ground black pepper.

2 Shape the lamb mixture with your hands into little fat sausages, about 5cm/2in long, and roll them in flour. Heat the olive oil in a frying pan.

3 Fry the sausages for about 8 minutes, turning them until evenly browned. Drain on kitchen paper.

4 Put the passata, sugar, bay leaves and whole onion in a pan and simmer for 20 minutes. Add the sausages and cook for 10 minutes. Take out the sausages and place on a serving dish, garnished with parsley.

COOK'S TIP
Passata is sieved tomato, which can be bought in cartons or jars.

LAMB FILO PIE

This recipe combines two popular ingredients: lamb and filo pastry. You can use chicken or fish too.

INGREDIENTS
sunflower oil, for brushing
450g/1lb/4 cups lean minced lamb
1 onion, sliced
1 garlic clove, crushed
400g/14oz can plum tomatoes
30ml/2 tbsp chopped fresh mint
5ml/1 tsp grated nutmeg
350g/12oz young spinach leaves
270g/10oz packet filo pastry
5ml/1 tsp sesame seeds
salt and freshly ground black pepper
salad or vegetables, to serve (optional)

SERVES 4

1 Preheat the oven to 200°C/400°F/Gas 6. Oil a 22cm/8½in round springform tin.

2 Fry the mince and onion without fat in a non-stick pan until golden. Add the garlic, tomatoes, mint, nutmeg and some seasoning. Bring to the boil whilst stirring, then simmer, stirring occasionally, until most of the liquid has evaporated.

3 Wash the spinach and remove any tough stalks, then cook in only the water clinging to the leaves for about 2 minutes, or until wilted.

4 Lightly brush each sheet of filo pastry with oil and lay in overlapping layers in the tin, leaving enough over-hanging to wrap over the top.

5 Spoon in the meat and spinach, then wrap the pastry over to enclose, scrunching it slightly. Sprinkle with sesame seeds and bake for about 25–30 minutes, or until golden and crisp. Serve hot, with salad or vegetables, if liked.

STUFFED TOMATOES AND PEPPERS

Colourful peppers and tomatoes make perfect containers for various meat and vegetable stuffings. This rice and herb version uses a variety of typically Greek ingredients.

INGREDIENTS
2 large ripe tomatoes
1 green pepper
1 yellow or orange pepper
60ml/4 tbsp olive oil, plus extra
for sprinkling
2 onions, chopped
2 garlic cloves, crushed
50g/2oz/¹/₂ cup blanched
almonds, chopped
75g/3oz/scant ¹/₂ cup long grain rice,
boiled and drained
15g/¹/₂oz fresh mint, roughly chopped
15g/¹/₂oz fresh parsley, roughly chopped
25g/1oz/2 tbsp sultanas
45ml/3 tbsp ground almonds
salt and freshly ground black pepper
chopped fresh herbs, to garnish

SERVES 4

1 Preheat the oven to 190°C/375°F/Gas 5. Cut the tomatoes in half and scoop out the pulp and seeds using a teaspoon. Leave the tomatoes to drain on kitchen paper with cut sides down. Roughly chop the tomato pulp and seeds.

2 Halve the peppers, leaving the cores intact, and scoop out the seeds. Brush the peppers with 15ml/1 tbsp of the olive oil and bake on a baking tray for 15 minutes. Place the pepper and tomato cases in a shallow ovenproof dish and season with salt and pepper.

3 Fry the onions in the remaining oil for 5 minutes. Add the garlic and chopped almonds and fry for 1 minute more.

4 Remove the pan from the heat and stir in the rice, chopped tomatoes, mint, parsley and sultanas. Season well with salt and pepper and spoon the mixture into the tomato and pepper cases.

5 Pour 150ml/¼ pint/⅔ cup boiling water around the tomatoes and peppers and bake, uncovered, in the preheated oven for 20 minutes. Scatter with the ground almonds and sprinkle with a little extra oil. Return to the oven and bake for a further 20 minutes, or until turning golden. Serve garnished with fresh herbs.

VARIATION
Small aubergines or large courgettes also make good vegetables for stuffing. Halve and scoop out the centres of the vegetables, then oil the vegetable cases and bake for about 15 minutes. Chop the centres, fry for 2–3 minutes to soften and add to the stuffing mixture. Fill the aubergine or courgette cases with the stuffing and bake as for the peppers and tomatoes.

AUBERGINE BAKE

The Greeks love to use aubergines in their cooking. Add some eggs and bake in the oven and you get a filling and delicious meal.

INGREDIENTS
60ml/4 tbsp oil
1 onion, finely chopped
3–4 garlic cloves, crushed
4 aubergines, cut lengthways into quarters
6 eggs
2–3 saffron strands, soaked in
15ml/1 tbsp boiling water
5ml/1 tsp paprika
salt and freshly ground black pepper
chopped fresh parsley, to garnish
herb bread and salad, to serve

SERVES 4

1 Preheat the oven to 180°C/350°F/Gas 4. Heat 30ml/2 tbsp of the oil in a frying pan and fry the onion until golden. Add the garlic and fry for about 2 minutes, then add the aubergines and cook for 10–12 minutes until soft and golden brown. Allow to cool and then chop the aubergines.

2 Beat the eggs in a large bowl and stir in the aubergine mixture, saffron water, paprika and seasoning (*left*). Place the remaining oil in a deep ovenproof dish. Heat in the oven for a few minutes, then add the egg and aubergine mixture. Bake for about 30–40 minutes until set. Garnish with chopped fresh parsley and serve with herb bread and a salad.

TOMATO AND OKRA STEW

O kra is an unusual and delicious vegetable. It releases a sticky sap when cooked, which helps to thicken this stew.

INGREDIENTS
15ml/1 tbsp olive oil
1 onion, chopped
400g/14oz can pimientos, drained
2 x 400g/14oz cans chopped tomatoes
275g/10oz okra
30ml/2 tbsp chopped fresh parsley
salt and freshly ground black pepper

SERVES 4

1 Heat the oil in a saucepan. Add the onion and cook for 2–3 minutes.

2 Using a small, sharp knife, roughly chop the drained pimientos and add them to the onion in the saucepan. Add the cans of chopped tomatoes and mix everything together thoroughly.

3 Cut the tops off the okra and add them to the pan. Season, then bring to the boil. Lower the heat, cover and simmer for about 12 minutes. Stir in the chopped parsley and serve at once.

BEAN STEW WITH VEGETABLES

A thick purée made up of cooked dried beans and vegetables is at the heart of this substantial stew called *fasolia*. It makes a warming winter lunch or supper dish.

INGREDIENTS

*350g/12oz/1½ cups dried cannellini
or other white beans
1 bay leaf
75ml/5 tbsp olive oil
1 onion, finely chopped
1 carrot, finely chopped
1 celery stick, finely chopped
3 tomatoes, peeled and finely chopped
2 garlic cloves, finely chopped
5ml/1 tsp fresh thyme leaves or
2.5ml/½ tsp dried thyme
salt and freshly ground black pepper
olive oil, to serve*

SERVES 6

1 Pick over the beans carefully, discarding any stones or other particles. Soak the beans in a large bowl of cold water overnight. Drain. Place the beans in a large saucepan of water, bring to the boil, and cook for 20 minutes. Drain. Return them to the pan, cover with cold water, and bring to the boil again. Add the bay leaf, and cook for about 1–2 hours, or until the beans are tender. Drain again, and remove the bay leaf from the mixture.

2 Purée about three-quarters of the drained beans in a food processor or blender, or pass through a food mill, adding a little water if necessary.

3 Heat the oil in a large pan. Stir in the onion, and cook until it softens. Add the carrot and celery and cook for 5 minutes.

4 Stir in the chopped tomatoes, garlic and thyme. Cook for 6–8 minutes more, stirring frequently.

5 Pour in 750ml/1¼ pints/3 cups boiling water. Stir in the beans and the bean purée. Season with salt and pepper. Simmer for 10–15 minutes. Serve in individual soup bowls, sprinkled with a little olive oil. Serve with chunks of fresh bread, if you like.

BROAD BEAN AND FETA SALAD

This recipe is loosely based on a typical medley of fresh-tasting Greek salad ingredients – broad beans, tomatoes and feta cheese. It is lovely when served warm or cold as a starter or main course accompaniment.

INGREDIENTS

900g/2lb broad beans, shelled, or
350g/12oz shelled frozen beans
60ml/4 tbsp olive oil
175g/6oz plum tomatoes, halved, or
quartered if large
4 garlic cloves, crushed
115g/4oz/1 cup firm feta cheese, cut
into chunks
45ml/3 tbsp chopped fresh dill
12 black olives
salt and freshly ground black pepper
chopped fresh dill, to garnish

SERVES 4–6

1 Cook the fresh or frozen broad beans in boiling, salted water until just tender. Drain and set aside.

2 Meanwhile, heat the oil in a heavy-based frying pan and add the tomatoes and garlic. Cook until the tomatoes are beginning to colour.

3 Add the feta cheese to the pan and toss the ingredients together for 1 minute. Mix with the drained beans, dill, olives and salt and pepper. Serve garnished with chopped dill.

GREEK SALAD

This classic salad, called *horiatiki*, is a wonderful combination of textures and flavours. The saltiness of the feta cheese is perfectly balanced by the variety of refreshing salad vegetables.

INGREDIENTS
1 cos lettuce heart
1 green pepper
1 red pepper
1/2 cucumber
4 tomatoes
1 red onion
225g/8oz/1 cup feta cheese, crumbled
black olives, to garnish

FOR THE DRESSING
45ml/3 tbsp olive oil
45ml/3 tbsp lemon juice
1 garlic clove, crushed
15ml/1 tbsp chopped fresh parsley
15ml/1 tbsp chopped fresh mint
salt and freshly ground black pepper

SERVES 4

1 Chop the lettuce into bite-size pieces. Seed the peppers, remove the cores and cut the flesh into thin strips. Chop the cucumber and slice or chop the tomatoes. Cut the onion in half, then slice finely.

2 Place the chopped lettuce, peppers, cucumber, tomatoes and onion in a large bowl. Scatter the feta over the top and toss together lightly.

3 To make the dressing for the salad, blend together the olive oil, lemon juice and garlic in a small bowl. Stir in the fresh parsley and mint and season with plenty of salt and pepper to taste.

4 Carefully pour the dressing over the salad and toss together lightly. Serve the salad in its bowl, garnished with a handful of black olives.

HALLOUMI AND GRAPE SALAD

Firm salty halloumi cheese is often served fried for breakfast or supper in Cyprus, where it originated from. In this recipe it is tossed with sweet, juicy grapes which really complement its distinctive flavour.

INGREDIENTS
150g/5oz mixed green salad leaves
75g/3oz seedless green grapes
75g/3oz seedless black grapes
250g/9oz halloumi cheese
45ml/3 tbsp olive oil
fresh young thyme leaves or dill,
to garnish

FOR THE DRESSING
60ml/4 tbsp olive oil
15ml/1 tbsp lemon juice
2.5ml/½ tsp caster sugar
15ml/1 tbsp chopped fresh thyme or dill
salt and freshly ground black pepper

SERVES 4

1 To make the dressing, mix together the olive oil, lemon juice and sugar. Season. Stir in the thyme or dill and set aside.

2 Toss together the salad leaves and the green and black grapes, then transfer to a large serving plate.

COOK'S TIP
Most large supermarkets sell ready-mixed bags of prepared salad leaves, which are ideal for use in this recipe. Experiment with various combinations to find the lettuce flavours that you like best.

3 Thinly slice the cheese. Heat the oil in a large frying pan. Add the cheese and fry briefly until turning golden on the underside. Turn the cheese with a fish slice and cook the other side.

4 Arrange the cheese over the salad. Pour over the dressing and garnish with thyme or dill.

SESAME SEED BREAD

Toasted sesame seeds give this bread its distinctive nutty flavour. The bread tastes good with savoury or sweet toppings.

INGREDIENTS
10ml/2 tsp dried yeast
pinch of sugar
175g/6oz/1½ cups plain flour
175g/6oz/1½ cups wholemeal flour
10ml/2 tsp salt
115g/4oz/½ cup toasted sesame seeds
milk, for glazing
25g/1oz/2 tbsp sesame seeds,
for sprinkling

MAKES 1 LOAF

1 Put 150ml/¼ pint/⅔ cup warm water in a jug. Sprinkle the yeast on top. Add the sugar, mix well and leave for 10 minutes.

2 Mix the flours and salt in a bowl. Make a well in the centre and pour in the yeast and 150ml/¼ pint/⅔ cup warm water.

3 With a wooden spoon, stir from the centre, incorporating flour with each turn, to obtain a rough dough.

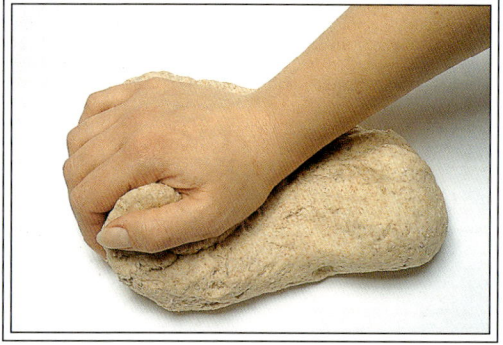

4 Transfer to a floured surface. To knead, push the dough away from you with the palm of your hand, then fold it towards you, and push away again. Repeat until smooth and elastic, return to the bowl and cover with a plastic bag. Leave in a warm place for 1½–2 hours until doubled in volume.

5 Grease a 23cm/9in cake tin. Punch down the dough and knead in the toasted sesame seeds.

6 Divide the dough into 17 balls and place in the prepared cake tin, making a loaf. Cover with a plastic bag and leave in a warm place until risen above the rim of the tin.

7 Preheat the oven to 220°C/425°F/Gas 7. Brush the top of the loaf with milk and sprinkle with the sesame seeds. Bake for 15 minutes. Lower the temperature to 190°C/375°F/Gas 5 and bake the loaf for about 30 minutes more until the bottom sounds hollow when lightly tapped. Cool on a wire rack, then serve.

OLIVE AND OREGANO BREAD

T his tasty bread is an excellent accompaniment to all salads and it is particularly good served warm.

INGREDIENTS
5ml/1 tsp dried yeast
pinch of sugar
15ml/1 tbsp olive oil
1 onion, chopped
450g/1lb/4 cups strong white flour
5ml/1 tsp salt
1.5ml/¼ tsp freshly ground black pepper
50g/2oz/½ cup stoned black olives,
roughly chopped
15ml/1 tbsp black olive paste
15ml/1 tbsp chopped fresh oregano
15ml/1 tbsp chopped fresh parsley

MAKES 1 LOAF

1 Put 150ml/¼ pint/⅔ cup warm water in a jug. Sprinkle the yeast on top. Add the sugar, mix well and leave for 10 minutes.

2 Heat the olive oil in a frying pan and fry the onion until golden brown.

3 Sift the flour into a mixing bowl with the salt and pepper. Make a well in the centre. Add the yeast mixture, the fried onion (with the oil), the black olives, olive paste, herbs and 150ml/¼ pint/⅔ cup warm water. Gradually incorporate the flour and mix to a soft dough, adding a little extra water if necessary.

4 Turn the dough on to a floured work surface and knead for 5 minutes until it is smooth and elastic. Place in a mixing bowl, cover with a damp dish towel and leave in a warm place to rise for about 2 hours until doubled in bulk. Lightly grease a baking sheet.

5 Turn the dough on to a floured work surface and knead again for a few minutes. Shape into a 20cm/8in round and place on the prepared baking sheet. Using a sharp knife, make criss-cross cuts over the top, cover and leave in a warm place for 30 minutes until well risen. Preheat the oven to 220°C/425°F/Gas 7.

6 Dust the loaf with a little flour. Bake for 10 minutes, then lower the temperature to 200°C/400°F/Gas 6. Bake for 20 minutes more, or until the loaf sounds hollow when it is tapped lightly underneath. Transfer the bread to a wire rack to cool slightly before serving it.

GREEK EASTER BREAD

In Greece, Easter celebrations are very important, and involve much preparation in the kitchen. This bread, known as *tsoureki*, is sold in all the baker's shops, and is also made at home. It is traditionally decorated with red dyed eggs and looks very attractive on the table.

INGREDIENTS
25g/1oz fresh yeast
120ml/4fl oz/½ cup warm milk
675g/1½lb/6 cups strong plain flour
2 eggs, beaten
2.5ml/½ tsp caraway seeds
15ml/1 tbsp caster sugar
15ml/1 tbsp brandy
50g/2oz/4 tbsp butter, melted
1 egg white, beaten
2–3 hard-boiled eggs, dyed red
50g/2oz/½ cup split almonds

MAKES 1 LOAF

COOK'S TIP
You can often buy fresh yeast from baker's shops. It should be pale cream in colour with a firm but crumbly texture.

1 Crumble the yeast into a bowl. Mix with 15–30ml/1–2 tbsp warm water until softened. Add the milk and 115g/4oz/1 cup of the flour. Mix, cover with a dish towel, and leave for 1 hour in a warm place.

2 Sift the remaining flour into a large bowl and make a well in the centre. Pour in the risen yeast and draw in a little of the flour. Add the eggs, caraway seeds, sugar, brandy and remaining flour to form a dough.

3 Mix in the melted butter. Turn on to a floured surface, and knead for about 10 minutes, until the dough becomes smooth. Return to the bowl, and cover with a dish towel. Leave in a warm place for about 3 hours to allow the dough to rise.

4 Preheat the oven to 180°C/350°F/Gas 4. Knock back the dough, turn it on to a floured surface and knead for 1–2 minutes. Divide the dough into three, and roll each piece into a long sausage. Make a plait as shown above, and place the loaf on a greased baking sheet.

5 Tuck the ends under, brush with the egg white and decorate with the eggs and split almonds. Bake for about 1 hour, until the loaf sounds hollow when tapped on the bottom. Cool on a wire rack and enjoy with your meal or even for breakfast with coffee.

NEW YEAR CAKE

A coin wrapped in foil is baked into this *vasilopitta* and tradition holds that good luck will come to the person who finds it.

INGREDIENTS
275g/10oz/2¹/₂ cups plain flour
10ml/2 tsp baking powder
50g/2oz/¹/₂ cup ground almonds
225g/8oz/1 cup butter, softened
175g/6oz/³/₄ cup caster sugar
4 eggs
150ml/¹/₄ pint/²/₃ cup fresh orange juice
50g/2oz/¹/₂ cup blanched almonds
15ml/1 tbsp sesame seeds

SERVES 8–10

1 Preheat the oven to 180°C/350°F/Gas 4. Grease a 23cm/9in square cake tin, line the base and sides with greaseproof paper and grease the paper.

2 Sift the flour and baking powder into a large mixing bowl and then stir in the ground almonds.

3 In another mixing bowl, cream together the butter and sugar until light and fluffy. Beat in the eggs, one at a time, using an electric mixer. Fold in the flour mixture, alternating with the orange juice, until evenly combined.

4 Add a coin wrapped in foil if you wish to make the cake in the traditional manner, then spoon the cake mixture into the prepared tin and smooth the surface. Arrange the almonds on top, then sprinkle over the sesame seeds. Bake in the centre of the oven for 50–55 minutes, or until a skewer inserted into the centre of the cake comes out clean. Leave to cool in the tin for about 5 minutes, then turn out on to a wire rack. Peel off the lining paper and leave the cake to cool completely. Serve cut into diamond shapes.

COOK'S TIP
This cake can be kept for up to four days in an airtight container.

HONEY AND LEMON CAKE

T his tangy cake makes a perfect mid-afternoon snack. Honey is used to sweeten many Greek dishes, and it adds its wonderful flavour to this cake.

INGREDIENTS
150g/5oz/1¼ cups plain flour
7.5ml/1½ tsp baking powder
2.5ml/½ tsp grated nutmeg
50g/2oz/⅓ cup semolina
2 egg whites
40g/1½oz/3 tbsp butter
60ml/4 tbsp clear honey
finely grated rind and juice of 1 lemon
150ml/¼ pint/⅔ cup milk
10ml/2 tsp sesame seeds

MAKES 16 SLICES

1 Preheat the oven to 200°C/400°F/Gas 6. Lightly grease a 19cm/7½in square deep cake tin and line the base with non-stick baking paper.

2 Sift together the flour, baking powder and nutmeg in a bowl, then beat in the semolina. Whisk the egg whites until they form soft peaks, then fold them evenly into the cake mixture.

3 Place the butter and 45ml/3 tbsp of the clear honey in a saucepan and heat gently until melted. Put aside 15ml/1 tbsp of the lemon juice, then stir the rest in the honey mixture along with the lemon rind and milk. Stir into the flour mixture.

4 Spoon the cake mixture into the tin and sprinkle with sesame seeds. Bake for 25–30 minutes, until golden brown. Mix the reserved honey and lemon juice and drizzle over the cake while warm. Cool in the tin, then cut into fingers to serve.

LOUKOUMIA

This is the Greek version of Turkish Delight and this versatile recipe can be made in minutes. Serve a few cubes with coffee after a heavy meal, for a pick-me-up. You can put cocktail sticks in each piece and decorate with a sprinkling of icing sugar.

INGREDIENTS
400g/14oz/2 cups sugar
300ml/½ pint/1¼ cups water
25g/1oz powdered gelatine
2.5ml/½ tsp cream of tartar
30ml/2 tbsp rose water
pink food colouring
45ml/3 tbsp icing sugar, sifted
15ml/1 tbsp cornflour

MAKES 450G/1LB

VARIATION
Try different flavours in this recipe, such as lemon, crème de menthe and orange and then vary the food colouring accordingly. For a truly authentic touch, add some chopped pistachio nuts to the mixture before pouring into the tins.

1 Wet the insides of two 18cm/7in shallow square tins with water. Place the sugar and all but 60ml/4 tbsp of the water in a heavy-based saucepan. Heat gently, stirring occasionally, until the sugar has dissolved.

2 Blend the gelatine and remaining water in a small bowl and place in a saucepan of hot water. Stir occasionally until dissolved.

3 Bring the sugar syrup to the boil and boil steadily for about 8 minutes until the syrup registers 130°C/260°F on a sugar thermometer. Stir the cream of tartar into the gelatine, then pour into the boiling syrup and stir until well blended. Remove from the heat.

4 Add the rose water and a few drops of pink food colouring to tint the mixture pale pink. Pour the mixture into the tins and allow to set for several hours or overnight.

5 Dust a sheet of waxed or greaseproof paper with some of the sugar and cornflour. Dip the base of the tin in hot water. Invert on to the paper. Cut into 2.5cm/1in squares using an oiled knife. Toss in icing sugar to coat.

FRUIT WITH YOGURT AND HONEY

F resh fruit most commonly follows a meal in Greece, and the addition of yogurt and honey makes it even more delicious.

INGREDIENTS

225g/8oz/1 cup Greek-style yogurt
45ml/3 tbsp clear honey
selection of fresh fruit for dipping, such as apples, pears, tangerines, grapes, figs and strawberries

SERVES 4

1 Beat the yogurt, place in a dish, and stir in the honey, to leave a marbled effect.

2 Cut the fruits into wedges or bite-size pieces, or leave whole.

3 Arrange the fruits on a platter with the bowl of dip in the centre. Serve chilled.

FIGS WITH HONEY AND WINE

Any variety of figs can be used in this recipe, their ripeness determining the cooking time. Choose ones that are plump and firm, and use quickly as they don't store well.

INGREDIENTS
450ml/³/₄ pint/scant 2 cups dry white wine
75g/3oz/¹/₃ cup clear honey
50g/2oz/¹/₄ cup caster sugar
1 small orange
8 whole cloves
450g/1lb fresh figs
1 cinnamon stick
mint sprigs or bay leaves, to decorate

FOR THE CREAM
300ml/¹/₂ pint/1¹/₄ cups double cream
1 vanilla pod
5ml/1 tsp caster sugar

SERVES 6

1 Put the wine, honey and sugar in a heavy-based saucepan and heat gently until the sugar dissolves.

2 Stud the orange with the cloves and add to the syrup with the figs and cinnamon. Cover and simmer gently for 5–10 minutes until the figs are softened. Transfer to a serving dish and leave to cool.

3 Put 150ml/¼ pint/⅔ cup of the cream in a small saucepan with the vanilla pod. Bring almost to the boil, then leave to cool and infuse for 30 minutes. Remove the vanilla pod and mix the flavoured cream with the remaining cream and sugar in a mixing bowl. Whip lightly. Transfer to a serving dish and serve with the figs.

BAKLAVA

his deliciously sticky pastry is popular all over Greece and across much of the Middle East.

INGREDIENTS
150g/5oz/²/₃ cup unsalted butter, melted
350g/12oz/3 cups ground pistachio nuts
150g/5oz/1¼ cups icing sugar
15ml/1 tbsp ground cardamom
450g/1lb filo pastry

FOR THE SYRUP
450g/1lb/2¼ cups sugar
30ml/2 tbsp rose water

SERVES 6–8

1 For the syrup, heat 300ml/½ pint/1¼ cups water with the sugar in a saucepan.

2 Bring to the boil and simmer for about 10 minutes until syrupy. Stir in the rose water and leave to cool.

3 Preheat the oven to 160°C/325°F/Gas 3. Brush a large rectangular baking tin with a little melted butter.

4 Mix together the ground pistachio nuts, icing sugar and cardamom to make the filling mixture.

5 Taking one sheet of filo pastry at a time, and keeping the remainder covered with a damp dish towel, brush with melted butter and lay on the bottom of the tin. Continue until you have six buttered layers in the tin. Spread half of the nut mixture over, pressing down with a spoon.

6 Take another six sheets of filo pastry, brush with butter, one by one, and lay over the nut mixture. Sprinkle over the remaining nuts and top with a final layer of six filo sheets brushed again with butter. Cut the pastry diagonally into small lozenge shapes using a sharp knife. Pour the remaining melted butter over the top.

7 Bake the pastries for 20 minutes, then increase the heat to 200°C/400°F/Gas 6 and bake for 15 minutes until light golden.

8 Remove from the oven and drizzle about three-quarters of the syrup over the pastry, reserving the remainder for serving. Leave to cool overnight and re-cut the pieces. Arrange the Baklava lozenges on a large glass dish, and serve with extra syrup.

INDEX